THINK
POSITIVE

Cope With Stress

Catherine Reef

TWENTY-FIRST CENTURY BOOKS
A DIVISION OF HENRY HOLT AND COMPANY • NEW YORK

Twenty-First Century Books
A Division of Henry Holt and Company, Inc.
115 West 18th Street
New York, NY 10011

Henry Holt ® and colophon are registered trademarks of
Henry Holt and Company, Inc.
Publishers since 1866

Published in Canada by Fitzhenry & Whiteside Ltd., 195 Allstate
Parkway, Markham, Ontario L3R 4T8

Library of Congress Cataloging-in-Publication Data
Reef, Catherine.
Think positive: cope with stress / Catherine Reef. — 1st ed.
p.   cm. — (Good health guidelines)
Includes index.
Summary: Discusses stress and how to manage it.
1. Stress (Psychology)—Juvenile literature. 2. Stress manage-
ment--Juvenile literature. [1. Stress (Psychology)
2. Stress management.] I. Title. II. Series
BF575.S75R37   1993
155.9'042--dc20   93-3973   CIP   AC

ISBN 0-8050-2443-3
First Edition 1993

Printed in the United States of America
All first editions are printed on acid-free paper ∞ .
10 9 8 7 6 5 4 3 2 1

Photo Credits
Cover: ©David Young-Wolff / PhotoEdit
p. 4: ©Richard Hutchings / Photo Researchers; p. 12: ©Dave Schaefer /
Monkmeyer Press; p. 20: ©Mimi Forsyth / Monkmeyer Press; p. 28: ©Jack
Sullivan Photography / Photo Researchers; p. 38: ©Richard Hutchings / Photo
Researchers; p. 48: ©Judith Aronson / Peter Arnold, Inc.; p. 56: ©Anne Sager /
Photo Researchers.

Contents

People who are mentally fit are people who like themselves.

1

A Healthy Outlook

The first days of September are a time for looking ahead. As the school year begins, young people think about what the coming months will bring. They're ready for learning and fun. "I'll be seeing my friends, meeting my new teachers, finding out my classes," says twelve-year-old Roshni, a middle school student.

J.K., ten, is eager to start science class. "I like mixing things together," he explains.

"I'm looking forward to being one year closer to graduating," jokes Diego, who is thirteen. Diego admits, however, that he hopes to try out for the school play, and he wonders what songs the chorus will be learning.

Like countless others, these children are able to enjoy life because they take good care of their health.

They get the exercise, good food, and sleep that their bodies need.

But good health means more than having a strong, fit body and being free of disease. It means having a healthy mind as well. People who are mentally fit are people who like themselves and who are proud of their achievements. They get along well with others at work and at play. They are able to get the most out of life.

People in good mental health have their share of ups and downs. At times, they experience worry and disappointment. No one can be on top of things all the time. These individuals, however, have learned to view their problems as challenges and to work to find solutions.

As the school year begins, students will meet new friends and take on new tasks. Some may find that their schoolwork is harder than it was the year before. Others will attend new schools where they will recognize few faces and must learn their way from room to room. Meeting these challenges will place demands on the the their bodies and minds. Like people of all ages, these boys and girls may experience the feeling called stress.

Stress is a response to the threats and hassles of everyday life. The muscles grow tense, and the heart beats faster. The person experiences a rush of energy.

He or she may feel worried or excited, fearful or even angry.

Many young people can sense when they are under stress. "Most of the times, my stomach starts to feel funny, and I kind of shiver a little bit," says Ashish, who is ten.

"It's like I get real hot for a minute," explains Nick, a fourth grader, "and it's all over my body."

Says fifteen-year-old Erin, "I get headaches. My head gets fuzzy, and I can't think."

"It's pressure," adds John, thirteen. "You are being torn apart."

Everyone needs some stress to keep life exciting. "It would get sort of boring if you just sat around all day and had no challenge," comments John's friend Andrew. A healthy amount of stress spurs you on to gain knowledge, maturity, and self-esteem. This good stress encourages you to do your best.

But for many people today, stress is chronic—they live with it day after day. People young and old have trouble making time for all of the things they need to do. Working at jobs all day and caring for their families creates stress for mothers and fathers. Many girls and boys hurry from school to jobs, sports activities, or music lessons. Others rush home to keep an eye on younger brothers and sisters. All of this activity, along with a heavy load of homework at night, is often stressful. The strain is even greater if a young person feels pressure to succeed.

Stress can have many causes, but some are more common than others. Children may feel fearful or uneasy about spending time alone at home after school. Young people often feel tension if they think that their classmates dislike them. For example, a girl may feel upset in physical education class if she is the last person chosen for a team. Or, a boy may be sad and angry if the popular students exclude him from their activities.

John remembers the stress he felt when he started the seventh grade. "I worried that I wouldn't fit in with everyone else and would feel like a geek," he explains.

Family problems, such as divorce, arguments, or financial worries, create stress for many children. The death of a parent or other loved one always causes painful feelings.

Stress can also come from changes, such as moving to a new town or city. Erin relates what it is like to enter high school, something that most teenagers look forward to. "It's all new—people who you don't know," she says. "It's really stressful at first because you don't know your way around and the teachers expect you to."

Stress can come simply from living in modern society. Children and adults must deal with such social problems as drug abuse, racism, poverty, and violence—often in their own neighborhoods.

Many young people name peer pressure as a common cause of stress. The desire to be popular with their peers, or others in their age group, often causes preteens and teens to choose a certain style of clothing or to listen to a particular kind of music.

Peer pressure becomes most stressful when young people feel pushed to do things they think are wrong or inappropriate for their age. For example, boys and girls may be urged to commit crimes or experiment with sex in order to fit in with certain groups.

A heavy load of stress strains the body's resources. In time, body systems can weaken, and illness can occur. Stress in adults has been linked to problems such as headaches, high blood pressure, heart disease, and even cancer. In children, it may lead to frequent stomachaches or headaches.

Young people under stress have a high number of colds, sore throats, and accidents. Some develop ailments such as stomach ulcers, which usually occur in adults. Stressed children and teens may also turn to alcohol and other drugs as they try to solve their problems. In doing so, they are breaking the law and harming their health.

A severe sign of stress in a child or teenager is the mental state known as depression. A person who is depressed feels sad for weeks or months at a time. He or she gets little enjoyment from life. In some cases, depression can lead to suicide. Anxiety is another mental health problem that sometimes results from stress. Someone who is anxious feels fear or panic in situations where there is no danger.

Many of the pressures of modern life are here to stay, but people don't need to suffer their harmful effects. There are ways to manage stress, methods that everyone can use to improve health and enjoy life more.

This book will show you how to stay mentally fit. It will help you understand stress and how it affects your life. You can use it as a tool to discover what is bothering you and how you are reacting. This book will also show you ways to control stress now and for the rest of your life. It will teach you to recognize depression and anxiety, and it will suggest ways to get help for these problems.

Mental fitness helps young people work well in school and enjoy their free time. It gives them confidence to make friends and enjoy good times with others. Good mental health makes it possible to live a full, active life.

The audition made him nervous...

2

The Stress Response

The school's hallway was filled with students. Some sang while others recited dramatic lines. "It was really noisy," Diego recalls. It was a cold December day, a day Diego had been waiting for since September. He and the others had come to try out for the school play.

The music teacher called the students into a quiet room in groups of three. Once inside, each boy or girl sang a song, and then the students read through a short scene together, to show their ability to act. The school would be presenting the musical play *Oliver*, about an orphan boy in England. The cast members had to be able to sing and act.

Diego sang a song that he had learned with the school chorus, a song called "Christmas Dreams." He remembers well how it felt to stand in front of others and sing by himself. "I had butterflies," he says, and he worried, "Will I stutter?" The audition made him nervous, "nervous enough that I was glad when it was over," he states.

These feelings—nervousness, worry, and fluttering stomach—are part of an age-old response. Diego reacted to the audition just as people have responded to challenges and dangers for thousands of years. His thoughts and sensations were part of the stress response.

Ever since prehistoric time, humans have confronted threats to their safety. Early people faced peril from wild animals and a harsh environment. The human race survived because these people had an inborn way of protecting themselves.

When an early human saw a wild animal or other possible danger, a portion of the brain called the cerebral cortex went to work. The cerebral cortex weighed the information coming in from the senses. If the person's safety appeared to be at risk, the cerebral cortex sent a message to the hypothalamus, an organ located below the brain. The hypothalamus, following orders, alerted the rest of the body to get ready for action.

In response to the warning from the hypothalamus, powerful chemicals called hormones flooded the system. One hormone, adrenaline, caused the breathing to quicken, so that more oxygen entered the system

14

from the air. It caused the heart to beat faster, delivering blood, rich with oxygen and nutrients, to the muscles and lungs. The adrenaline also made the person more alert. Another hormone, endorphin, acted as a natural painkiller. It allowed the person to remain active even if an injury occurred.

Other changes took place in the body as well. The digestive system shut down, sending most of its blood supply to the muscles, heart, and lungs. As the blood rushed to where it was most needed, the person's skin grew pale and sweaty. Sugar and cholesterol entered the bloodstream to provide a steady energy supply. The senses of sight, hearing, taste, touch, and smell grew sharper, enabling the person to notice any possible sign of danger.

Together, these changes are called the stress response. They helped early humans prepare for "fight or flight." The ancestors of modern people had to be ready to fight against the threats they faced or to run away from them. Once the danger passed, their bodies and minds returned to their normal, relaxed state.

Something that threatens a person's safety or feeling of well-being is called a stressor. And although the people of the 1990s face stressors very different from the threats of prehistoric time, their bodies respond in the same way. People still experience a rush of hormones, rapid breathing, a quickened heartbeat, changes in blood flow, high blood levels of sugar and cholesterol, and increased alertness. "It makes you feel like your heart's going to blow up," John remarks.

"Fight or flight" protected people long ago, but it does not work well against the threats that people face today. The fight-or-flight response offered no help to Diego as he tried out for the school play. It is useless to you if you have too much to do, if your family is moving, or if you have a disagreement with your friend. Running from the room will not solve a dispute. And how can you do battle with a busy schedule?

A run-in with a wild animal might have lasted only a few minutes, but modern stressors tend to be long lasting. The upset resulting from divorce, for example, can cause stress for years. Also, people today often live with more than one stressor—perhaps family problems in combination with school pressure and shyness about making friends. Instead of returning to normal, modern bodies and minds often remain in a state of alertness, constantly ready for fight or flight.

When the human body is continually responding to stress, health suffers. Over time, the high levels of hormones in the blood can cause shakiness and make it hard to fall asleep. They can break down the body's ability to fight illness. A disturbed digestive system can result in nausea, diarrhea, and cramps. A high level of cholesterol in the blood puts people at risk for heart disease in later life. A continually rapid heart-beat may raise the risk of heart disease, too. It can also lead to high blood pressure.

A Canadian researcher, Dr. Hans Selye, observed that the stress response occurs in three stages. He called the three together the General Adaptation Syndrome. Stage one, said Selye, is "Alarm." In this stage, the body reacts to a threat, or stressor. The body prepares for fight or flight.

Selye called stage two "Resistance." This is the stage in which the body tries to adapt to the stressful situation. One of the body's organs or systems may take over the struggle in this stage. The muscles may remain tense, for example, or poor digestion may persist.

Stage three, "Exhaustion," results from living with stress for weeks, months, or years. Because both the body and the mind are exhausted in this stage, physical and mental health problems can occur. With a tired body and a worried mind, a person pays less attention to safety. Someone in stage three of the General Adaptation Syndrome is at a high risk for accidents and injuries.

People don't need to wait until they reach stage three to realize that they are carrying a heavy stress load. Instead, they can learn to recognize stress's warnings. Those under stress often find it hard to relax or have fun. They may get angry easily, perhaps over little things. Stress can make people feel that they are always in a hurry or that they have too much to do.

Also, a common symptom is to have trouble concentrating and maybe to spend lots of time daydreaming. Some people react by feeling tired or worn out much of the time.

"Another sign of stress could be if you see everything in a negative view, if you don't see anything positively," Andrew observes.

If you have any of these warning signs, you need to look carefully at your life to find the causes of stress. You can then learn ways to handle the stress, to protect your health and increase your enjoyment of life.

Diego's audition took only a few minutes, but his stress lasted longer. "The worst part was waiting to find out if I got the part," he explains. Diego tried out just before the Christmas break. He had to wait until January, when school began again, to learn what his teacher had decided.

Back in school, Diego saw a group of students clustered around a notice on the wall, a list of those chosen for the play. "I looked at the cast list, and I found out that I had gotten the part," he says. The stress of waiting was over. But now, as rehearsals start, Diego faces new obstacles. "I'm mostly worried about acting," he confesses, "because I've never acted in a play before."

Yet Diego is confident that he has the time and talent to meet this new challenge. "The play is still about three months away," he says. "I'm getting better at saying my lines every day."

Stress occurs when you are afraid you are not going to do well on a test.

3

The Stressors in Your Life

The first step in getting mentally fit is learning what causes the stress response in you.

Many stressors have something in common: They involve change. A change in someone's habits, family, or way of life is often stressful because the person must adapt, or get used to the change.

Dr. Thomas Holmes and Dr. Richard Rahe, two researchers at the University of Washington School of Medicine, spent twenty years studying the effects of important life changes on health. They discovered that such changes as the death of a loved one, divorce, or a move were all causes of stress. Even welcome changes, like a new baby in the family or a long-awaited vacation, also can be stressful, the scientists found, because people still have to adapt.

Holmes and Rahe's research showed that the more changes a person experiences within a twelve-month period, the greater the risk of getting a stress-related illness within the next two years.

Major life events are difficult for all people, but they are not the only causes of stress. For Nick, stress comes from being late, "when I'm on a bike ride and I'm supposed to be back at a certain time, but it's past that time," he explains. "Mom gets mad if I'm late, even if I'm a minute late. And I usually don't wear watches."

Stress occurs for J.K. at school, "when you are afraid you are not going to do well on a test."

Someone else might take being late in stride or might breeze through a test free of worry. The reason is that stress frequently results from how a person perceives an event, not from the event itself. What is threatening to one may not be threatening to all.

People commonly create stress in their imaginations. For instance, everyone loves to hear John play the piano, and he's often called upon to play at home and at school. But even before he sits down on the bench, John starts listening to a little voice in his mind, telling him that he will play poorly. "I hope I don't mess up," he worries. John pictures his fingers hitting the wrong keys, and he feels the stress response—even though he hasn't played a note. His poor performance takes place only in his mind.

How can negative thinking cause stress? The answer lies in the fact that the body cannot tell the difference between an event that really happens and one that occurs in the imagination. The body reacts to all stressors in the same way, with rapid breathing, tight muscles, fear, and other aspects of the fight-or-flight response.

People differ in the way they handle life's challenges, too. Scientists have found that those who are least affected by stress possess a trait called hardiness. They share a set of health-protecting qualities. These people welcome the change that life brings, seeing it as a chance for learning and new experiences. They feel a sense of commitment and that their lives have a purpose, or that they are working toward a goal. Hardy individuals sense that they are in control of their lives—events do not control them.

Self-esteem offers protection against stress, too. Children and adults who feel good about themselves and their abilities are willing to accept challenges. As they seek new experiences, they are able to risk failure for the chance to achieve.

There are others, in contrast, who perceive that whatever happens is beyond their control. They may resist any kind of change. These people tend to suffer the strongest effects of stress. As a result, they face a high risk of stress-related health problems.

No one enjoys feeling worried or pressured. It's common to try to get rid of the unpleasant feelings brought on by the fight-or-flight response. Some children and adults deal with stress in harmful ways. They may lose their temper or engage in loud or rude behavior, causing anger or hurt feelings in others. They may rush through their work and make mistakes. They may eat junk food, smoke, or use alcohol or other drugs and so risk damaging their health. Others try to bottle up their feelings—only to have them burst forth later on.

Other responses may not cause harm, but they do nothing to help the stressful situation. "I ignore it, leave it alone," John says. Some days, Nick goes outside to kick trees.

Does the stress in your life result from change or from other causes? Is it produced in your imagination? How are you responding to that stress?

The way to learn what is causing stress for you—and how you are reacting—is to keep a Stress Diary. For three or four days, note all of the times when you feel stressed. For each event that you observe, write down the date, the time of day, and the stressor.

Also, observe your body, mind, and behavior so that you can list how you reacted. Did you feel tense muscles or a rapid heartbeat? Did you develop a headache or an upset stomach? Was it hard for you to relax? Did you worry or daydream? Were your actions rushed and careless?

Here are some of the kinds of entries a young person might make in a Stress Diary.

Sample Stress Diary

Day	Time	Stressor (cause of stress)	Reaction
Mon.	9 A.M.	Forgot to do science homework	Rapid heartbeat, quick breathing, worry that teacher will be angry
Mon.	3 P.M.	Tryouts for basketball team	Stomach cramps, afraid that I will mess up
Mon.	8 P.M.	Argument with sister over which TV show to watch	Angry, tense, sulked in room all evening
Tues.	10:30 A.M.	Math test	Headache, tense muscles
Tues.	3 P.M.	Learned I made the team	Happy, but headache worsens
Tues.	9:15 P.M.	Overheard parents talking about the rent and bills	Worry about the family, trouble falling asleep
Wed.	7:15 A.M.	Argument with sister because she wore my new jacket	Angry, hurt because Mom refused to stick up for me
Wed.	9 A.M.	Left book report home	Rapid heartbeat, quick breathing
Wed.	3–8 P.M.	Busy schedule: basketball practice, shopping, help start dinner, homework	Tense muscles, headache, tired but hard to fall asleep at night

After keeping your Stress Diary, you may find that some of your stressors are similar to those listed. You probably noticed several others as well. When your diary is complete, you are ready to design a mental fitness program, an organized plan for lowering the amount of stress in your life.

Trying to deal with all of your stress at once would be a big job—one that would be hard to do well. It's better to focus on the two or three stressors that are having the greatest impact on your life. These are the ones that occur most often or that cause you the most difficulty. Your Stress Diary can help you see which ones they are.

Once you know your major stressors, list them on a piece of paper, skipping lines. Beneath each one, set yourself a goal— describe the situation or event as you would like it to be.

Here are some examples of stressors and goals based on the Stress Diary included in this chapter:

Stressor #1: Forgetting assignments

Goal #1: I remember to do my assignments at night and to bring them to school in the morning.

Stressor #2: Arguments with sister

Goal #2: My sister and I decide things together instead of fighting to get our own way.

Your mental fitness program is a way to reach these goals. It is an organized plan that uses healthful methods to reduce stress. When your goals have been achieved, you can go on to tackle some of the other stressors that you have identified.

Stressors don't have to harm your health and ability to do well. There are things you can do to lessen their effects. You may actually be able to change or eliminate some stressors. You may find ways to avoid some others. There are also methods to make yourself more resistant to stress.

Having someone to listen helps you know that you are not facing problems alone...

4

Making Changes

Andrew remembers, "I had a week and a half when everything I did wouldn't go right. I would do my homework and then accidentally leave it on the table at home. I was going to someone's house to spend the night. Then I got sick at the last minute and couldn't go." This run of bad luck was stressful for Andrew, and he needed to get his feelings off his chest.

Andrew found two willing listeners in his family. "I talked about it with Mom and Dad for a while," he remarks. Andrew told his parents that he felt low, that nothing was going right. And when he finished, he realized that life looked brighter. "There was really no solution. It was just dumb luck. But you've got to deal with that and do the best you can," he concludes. "You just talk about it and get it out of your system."

Having someone to listen helps you know that you are not facing problems alone, that another person understands. "Unexpressed feelings are like splinters," states Donald Wiczer, M.D., a pediatrician in Washington, D.C. A splinter left beneath the skin can cause pain, redness, and even infection. Troubling thoughts that are held inside can fester, too, causing growing amounts of stress and upset. Both splinters and worries need to come out.

For this reason, an important step in managing stress is to talk with a parent or other caring adult about the things that are on your mind. Talking things over can change how you perceive, or view, the events in your life. You will probably learn that your feelings are not unusual. Everyone has times of stress.

The adult may offer advice about solving your problems. Also, because the adults in a family are often in charge of the children's schedules, they can help reduce the stress that comes from having too much to do. As Kenneth Cooper, M.D., a well-known expert on health and fitness, explains, "Parents have the most control over the degree of stress that their children must face."

Many young people prefer to discuss their worries with friends. The adults in their home may seem too busy to listen. They may show little understanding. Friends can offer a sympathetic ear and, sometimes, good advice. But adults have more maturity and life experience. They are better equipped for handling life's difficulties. If you can't talk to an adult at home, find a teacher, school counselor, or other man or woman who is willing to listen and help.

As you plan your mental fitness program, it will help to show your Stress Diary to a parent or other adult. Explain what you want to do. You and the adult can then work as partners to reduce your stress.

The easiest way to ease your stress load may be to avoid, or even get rid of, some of its causes. Let's say a girl feels stressed when doing her homework because noise from the television distracts her. She could remedy this problem in a number ofs ways. She might ask the other family members to turn down the volume when she is studying. Another solution would be to do her homework at a different time of day. Or, she could take her books to her room and close the door so that she had a quiet place to work.

People can also do away with the stress they create in their own minds. These are the imagined threats, such as John's "messed up" piano playing. They are events that cause stress even though they may never happen. You can end this kind of stress with a technique called "thought stopping." Whenever you start listening to the inner voice that whispers negative thoughts, tell yourself, "Stop!" Then replace the unwanted thoughts with positive ones.

John could reduce the stress he feels before a performance by stopping his mental voice and replacing its messages with helpful thoughts. He might tell himself, "I have practiced this music many times, and I know I can play it well. The audience is sure to enjoy my playing." Another useful thought might be, "Even if I hit a wrong note, I can still finish the song."

It is possible, too, for John to use his imagination in a positive way. He could imagine himself playing very well and picture the happy faces of his classmates or family. Then he could focus on making this positive image come true.

And each successful performance will improve John's self-esteem. Listening to his audience applaud, he will feel a sense of accomplishment. Each success will make him better able to face new situations with minimal stress.

It's your accomplishments that help boost your self-esteem. Whenever you develop a skill or do something that you have not done before, you gain confidence in your abilities. You learn to like yourself a little better and you overcome stress.

A high level of self-esteem will help you resist peer pressure. Others will notice your confidence and seek your friendship. They may even try to be more like you!

Many people ease the stress of a busy schedule by learning to manage their time. When they make good decisions about how they will use their day, they can do more of the things they want to do—without the stress of feeling rushed.

You, too, can manage your time. Start by making a list of everything you plan to do in the week ahead. When your list is complete, you will see that some of the tasks you wrote down are more important than others. Look over your list and mark a "1" beside the items that are most important and a "2" by those that come next in importance. Write "3" alongside the items on your list that are low in importance, and cross out any that you can probably skip.

You will then plan your schedule for the coming week, setting aside enough time for the activities numbered "1" and "2." This strategy will help you avoid a crunch, for example, when you have a report to complete for school. Plan to do the activities numbered "3" only if you have time left over.

Think whether other people can help with some of your duties. And be sure to schedule time to relax and have fun. Such a plan will make you happier and more alert and give you more energy for the important tasks.

Good communication is another key to stress management. Stress often results when people disagree or fail to understand one another. Nick and Erin, who are brother and sister, know this all too well. "She's always annoying me," Nick complains. "She's always playing my games. She doesn't let me play with them all day."

Erin has a gripe of her own. "He always has to have his way about everything." By practicing communication skills, this pair could reduce the strife in their relationship and ease some of their stress. You can apply these skills as well as you interact with others.

One communication skill, careful listening, will help you understand what people are really trying to say. Being a good listener means setting aside your own thoughts to focus on the speaker's message. Sometimes people appear to be listening, but are really thinking about what they will say next. It's easy for them to miss something that was said.

If you are not sure that you understand what the speaker is trying to say, ask questions. It often helps to restate the message in your own words, so the person can correct anything you failed to understand.

Also, listen with your eyes as well as your ears. Watch people's "body language" to see if their expressions or movements tell you anything. For example, tapping fingers might mean, "I'm nervous." A bouncing step might be telling you, "I'm feeling happy and carefree." A wrinkled forehead often means, "I'm concentrating" or, "I'm concerned." It's helpful to observe the faces and actions of the people around you in order to decide what unspoken messages they convey.

Asserting yourself is another communication skill. To assert yourself means to stand up for your rights or state your feelings. Many people find this hard to do. But when they keep their opinions to themselves, they fail to solve their problems. They also feel stress. Others take an aggressive approach. In order to get their own way, they trample on other people's rights and feelings. Anger and stress are the result. Being assertive lets you respect other people as well as yourself.

Speaking assertively involves three steps. First, say something to show the other person that you understand his or her point of view. Second, sum up the problem as you see it. Third, suggest a solution that you and the other person can accept.

Assertiveness can be an effective response to peer pressure. You may wish to practice responding to pressure with a family member or friend.

Here are some assertive statements that Nick and Erin could use to improve the way they get along:

"Erin, I can see that you like to play with my game. You have had it all afternoon, though, and I want a turn. Suppose you use it for a few more minutes and then give me a chance to play."

"Nick, I know that you had planned to watch a TV show tonight. But there is a movie coming on that I really want to see. If you agree to watch the movie tonight, I'll be happy to let you choose our shows on Friday and Saturday."

When you and another person disagree, remember that there does not have to be a "winner" or a "loser." It's possible to resolve the conflict in a way that allows both people to win. After giving yourselves time to calm down, you and the other person may wish to "brainstorm"—to list every possible way to solve your dispute, no matter how farfetched some of the ideas may seem. You just might come up with something that works. If the two of you cannot talk calmly about your differences, you might prefer to speak with a third person who is objective, who can approach the issue fairly and without emotion.

You now know several ways to change or get rid of stressors. These include changing your perceptions, or the way you think about stressful events; stopping negative thoughts; building self-esteem; managing time; and learning to communicate. Would these methods work for any of your major stressors? If so, make them part of your mental fitness plan.

Some sources of stress cannot be changed or avoided. Stressors such as a grandparent's illness or a tough school subject are here to stay. To deal with these, you will need another set of skills—skills to reduce stress's harmful effects.

An activity that lets you work with your hands...can be especially soothing.

5

Living Well With Stress

Many people who are under stress feel that they can't wind down. Day and night, their minds stay busy with worries. Their bodies remain tense and primed for action. "How can I relax," they ask themselves, "when I have so much to do?"

Yet these busy people can usually do just as much—and also feel better—if they take the time to loosen up. When someone is relaxed, the mind is clear and peaceful, the heart rate and breathing slow down, and the muscles let go of their tension.

A relaxed state is the opposite of the stress response. Because you cannot be stressed and relaxed at the same time, you can protect your health by taking a breather.

There are many ways to relax. Some people unwind by taking up a hobby. An activity that lets you work with your hands, such as drawing, building models, sewing, or raising plants, can be especially soothing. "I love reading," Nick says. Getting swept up in a good book helps to clear the mind and loosen the muscles.

Spending pleasant time with friends is a great way to relax and lower stress. "Sometimes you can talk about whatever's on your mind with other people," Roshni notes. Your friends may have faced similar problems and be able to offer advice. You can laugh and have fun with the people you like. You may even wish to enjoy a new activity with a friend or family member. The possibilities are endless. You could visit a museum together, try out some recipes, join a team, or sign up for a class.

Quiet time calms people, too, so it's wise to seek some every day. You may wish to spend some moments alone, perhaps thinking peaceful thoughts, listening to music, taking a bath, or writing a letter to someone far away. It may relax you to pass some time with your pet.

Laughter is something else that soothes the body and mind. When people laugh heartily, the muscles in their arms and legs go limp. When they stop laughing, the rest of their muscles relax. Their heart rate and blood pressure drop.

There is an old saying that "laughter is the best medicine." Sharing a laugh with other people is certainly an enjoyable way to lower stress and protect your health. "I like jokes—like John's life," Andrew says, teasing his friend. "Sometimes I watch a comedy show," comments Roshni.

If you enjoy seeing funny movies or reading humorous books, make time for those activities. It may even help you to remember something comical that happened in the past.

Many people manage stress through a practice called controlled relaxation. In a quiet, comfortable place, free from distractions, they rid their bodies and minds of tension. They concentrate on a single word or phrase in order to let go of negative thoughts and worries. As they imagine a peaceful scene, such as a beach or garden, they release the tightness in their muscles. Their heart rate and breathing slow down. Some children and adults listen to cassette tapes that guide them into deeper and deeper states of relaxation.

Ashish learned a relaxation exercise at school. It's a simple method he can use anytime, anywhere. "Breathe in from your nose for three seconds, then breathe out for five seconds," he explains. "Do that a few times, and that will calm you down."

While relaxing combats the stress response, being in good physical shape offers protection from the harmful effects of stress. People under pressure would be smart to take very good care of their bodies.

Research has shown that those who are physically fit have milder reactions to stress than others who are in poor shape. Exercisers have strong muscles and joints. They have improved their endurance—the ability to stay active at work and play.

Exercise also tends to bring on a relaxed, happy feeling. Roshni, who belongs to a swim team, has had this experience. "Sometimes swimming can help," she says. "It gets your mind off things. You concentrate more on your swimming."

J.K. has calmed himself on the baseball diamond. "Once I was really mad, so it was great hitting a ball," he recalls. "I didn't really feel mad after that."

The improved mood that exercise brings can last for two hours or more. And getting fit helps people feel better about themselves and more in control of their lives.

The best kind of exercise to choose is something that is aerobic. Aerobic activities involve steady movement. They cause the body to use lots of oxygen. They strengthen the heart and lungs as well as the muscles. Biking, rapid walking, jogging, running, and swimming can all provide aerobic benefits.

Aerobic exercise does the most good when it is performed for twenty to thirty minutes, at least three times a week. So that your body has time to get used to a higher level of activity, begin each aerobic workout with a "warm-up"—five minutes of slow exercise and stretching. And when your workout is over, a "cool down" will give your body a chance to adjust to a slower pace. During these five minutes, exercise at a reduced rate and then gently stretch the muscles you have used.

People under stress can also protect their health by eating balanced, nutritious meals. At busy, hectic times, it's tempting to skip meals or reach for fast food. But this eating style fails to provide all of the nourishment that the body needs. And many snacks and fast-food items are high in sugar, fat, and sodium. Over time, this kind of diet can lead to obesity (being 20 percent or more above recommended weight). It can help to cause heart disease, high blood pressure, diabetes, and other health problems in later life.

How do you eat a healthful diet, one that meets all of the body's nutritional needs? You can begin by choosing a variety of foods from all of the food groups. The U.S. Department of Agriculture recently organized those groups into a "food pyramid" to help everyone make healthful choices.

Nutrition experts advise people to select most of their foods from the groups in the larger blocks near the pyramid's base: breads and cereals, vegetables, and fruit. All of these foods contain the nutrients known as vitamins and minerals, which the body needs in very small amounts.

Bread, cereal, pasta, and other foods made from grain are high in carbohydrates, the body's main source of energy. Fruits, vegetables, and whole-grain products are sources of dietary fiber, the part of plants that the body cannot digest. Fiber keeps the digestive system functioning well by moving food through the body.

Higher up on the food pyramid are dairy products and the protein-rich foods—meat, fish, and dried beans and peas. Milk and other dairy foods are the best sources of calcium, a mineral needed for strong bones and teeth. The human body uses the protein from meat, fish, and beans to build all of its tissues, from muscles and skin to internal organs and hair. The pyramid blocks containing these two food groups are smaller, as a warning that some of these foods are high in fat.

The smallest block, up at the top of the pyramid, holds fats, oils, and sweets. The foods in this group include butter, margarine, cooking oil, shortening, candy, syrups, and soft drinks. These foods offer few nutrients but lots of sugar and fat. It's best to use them sparingly or to make healthful choices instead. In place of candy, cookies, or other sweets, reach for fresh fruit, yogurt, or a slice of hearty bread. Low-fat milk or fruit juice is a more nutritious thirst quencher than soda.

To cut down on fat, eat foods that are baked, broiled, or steamed, rather than fried in oil or grease. Choose low-fat and skim milk products. Before cooking, remove the white fat from meat and the fatty skin from chicken.

Most of the sodium that people eat comes from table salt. So, an easy way to eat less sodium is to stop using the salt shaker at meals. Salty snacks, such as potato chips and pretzels, tend to be high in sodium, so it's wise to munch on salt-free treats, like plain popcorn or fresh vegetables. It may take time, but you can get used to the taste of food without salt.

There are several other things you can do to protect your health. First, make sure that you get enough sleep. The amount of sleep that young people require declines slowly between the ages of six and sixteen, dropping from eleven to eight hours each night. Boys and girls age ten to fourteen need nine to ten hours of sleep nightly.

Next, be sure to have medical checkups according to the schedule your doctor recommends, along with any needed immunizations. Finally, if you have been coping with stress in a harmful way, perhaps by smoking or overeating, it's time to adopt healthful methods instead. You will need professional help, however, for a problem of drug or alcohol abuse. To take the first step, talk with a parent, school counselor, doctor, or other health professional.

You may never rid your life of stressors, but you can keep them from getting the best of you. Seek out peace through hobbies or quiet time, laughter or controlled relaxation. Spend time with the people you enjoy. And build a healthy, stress-resistant body through exercise and good nutrition. There's so much you can do to protect your health.

Living with depression is
like living under a dark, dreary cloud.

6

When Help Is Needed

When stress is severe or long lasting, the state of mind and body called depression can result. Living with depression is like living under a dark, dreary cloud. You feel sad and empty inside, and may care little about how you look to others. You might think you are the only person who has ever felt this way. Unable to find any pleasure in life, you lose interest in activities you once enjoyed.

Someone who is depressed may adopt new, harmful behavior, perhaps skipping school or even running away. When depression is severe, a young person may try to get rid of unhappy feelings with drugs or alcohol. Some try to take their own lives. Because depression is a serious problem, people who are depressed need care from a qualified therapist.

Mental health experts have identified a group of symptoms to help them diagnose the disorder called clinical depression. These include lasting feelings of sadness, emptiness, or hopelessness; trouble concentrating or making decisions; and being unable to enjoy daily activities, possibly dropping out of clubs or teams. Depressed children and teens often have trouble getting along with others at school or at home. They are likely to lack energy and to show changes in their sleep patterns and eating habits. They may sleep either too much or too little; they may either overeat or lose their appetites and skip meals.

The list of symptoms continues. Headaches, stomachaches, and other ailments become common. These young people avoid their friends and spend a great deal of time alone. They may become heavy drinkers or drug users. Some speak of suicide, either seriously or in the form of jokes.

Depression may follow a major life change, such as a parent losing a job or the death of a loved one. But sometimes it is hard to pinpoint the reason for the depressed feelings. They simply are there. At times, depression results from physical causes. Also, the disorder occurs more often in some families than in others.

Depression affects people of all ages. It occurs in men and women, boys and girls. According to the National Institute of Mental Health, as many as 3 percent to 5 percent of teenagers will feel depressed in a single year. "That means that among 100 friends, four could be clinically depressed," the institute advises.

Anxiety is another mental health problem that commonly occurs in people under stress. Those suffering from anxiety feel controlled by fear. Day after day, they live with the physical and mental effects of fright—a racing heart, tense muscles, panicky thoughts— even though they face little or no danger.

Phobias are a second kind of anxiety disorder. Someone with a phobia fears a specific object or situation that most people do not find threatening. The fear of flying and the fear of snakes are common phobias.

Some anxious individuals avoid certain places or situations that they believe bring on their anxiety. An anxious young person may try to stay home from school, for example. It's easy to see how anxiety prevents people from leading full, active lives. Also, this constant fearfulness places a great demand on the body. Someone with an anxiety disorder is at a high risk for a stress-related illness.

As with depression, the causes of anxiety are sometimes not clear. Although anxiety often occurs in people who are highly stressed, it may also have a physical cause. Caffeine—a chemical found in coffee, tea, and some soft drinks—can trigger anxiety in certain individuals. Some experts think that phobias might result from bad experiences. A young child who is frightened by nighttime thunder, for example, may grow up to be fearful of electrical storms. Other experts link phobias to an overactive imagination.

Although self-help measures can reduce ordinary stress, people suffering from anxiety and depression benefit most from professional help. A psychologist, clinical social worker, or psychiatrist can provide the needed therapy.

All of these men and women have had years of training. They know how to help people understand their feelings and solve their problems. Psychiatrists are medical doctors, which means they can also prescribe medicines to those who need them.

Your doctor or a school counselor can help you and your family find a therapist who has experience working with young people. This kind of treatment need not be expensive. Community mental health agencies often provide counseling services, and they base their fees on a family's ability to pay.

The therapist will want to learn as much as possible about you and your family. Most likely, he or she will meet with the members of your family in a group or by themselves. The therapist will ask numerous questions. It is important to answer honestly and completely so the therapist obtains all of the information he or she needs.

The therapist may suggest that you have a medical examination, to learn whether there is a physical cause for the psychological symptoms.

Depression and anxiety tend to improve quickly once therapy starts. Therapists work to help young people find healthful ways to cope with stressful situations. In counseling sessions, children and teens learn to have self-confidence and to think well of themselves. They learn how to change any behavior that is causing difficulty. The therapist and the young person may also work together on interpersonal skills, such as ways to make friends or get along with others. Quite often, family members learn new ways to interact.

Sometimes the therapist will suggest that the boy or girl take medication to ease unpleasant symptoms. If he or she cannot prescribe medicines, the therapist will refer the patient to a physician who can.

But what do you do if it is not you, but a friend, who shows signs of a mental health problem? It can be deeply troubling when a friend seems anxious or depressed, especially if the friend talks of suicide. Young people often wonder whether they should tell someone. Would they be revealing a secret that their friend has told them in confidence?

Speaking up, experts agree, is the wisest action to take. It's best to tell a trusted adult, such as a parent or teacher, about the situation. The adult can then talk to the troubled young person or his or her family and see that help is obtained.

As one teenager who lost a friend to suicide explained, "You can't talk a depressed person into being happy. They need professional help." Telling an adult is a true act of friendship. It can even save a life.

People with problems like depression and anxiety commonly feel shy about seeking professional help. They worry that no one will understand their feelings or that others will think they are crazy. These children and adults need to understand, however, that the stresses of life can overwhelm anyone. Their symptoms are normal responses to difficult situations.

Also, everyone feels depressed or anxious at times. Many people, including parents, teachers, and schoolchildren, have sought counseling. No one is ever alone. Caring people are waiting to help.

A healthy way of life will provide...plenty of energy to do the things you want to do.

7

A Lifelong Task

Childhood, adolescence, adulthood—every age brings new experiences. In the years ahead, the students in elementary schools will enter junior high and high school. They may then go to college or sign up for military service. In time, they will start careers. Many will marry and have children of their own.

"I guess I want to go on to college," says Erin.

Roshni plans to be a lawyer, "because she's so good at arguing," her mother remarks.

"I'd like to be a cameraman, a TV reporter, or an architect," Diego says. "I like to design houses."

All of these experiences will involve learning and challenge—and they will also bring stress. As life goes on, today's young people will face disappointments and setbacks. These unhappy events will cause stress, too. They may bring on the unpleasant symptoms of depression or anxiety. That's why staying mentally fit is a task that continues for life.

By reading this book you have gained knowledge that will help you feel in control of your life. You have learned to recognize the stress response, and you know how it affects health. You have seen how stress places demands on the body and keeps people from doing their best. You have also picked up important skills, skills you can use to protect your well-being.

If you completed a Stress Diary, you identified the problems and events that are causing stress for you right now. You may already have taken steps to ease some of the pressure. But managing stress is not something to do only once. Life will continue to surprise you with changes and difficulties. That's why it's a good idea, as the months and years pass, to make regular checks on the stress in your life. One way to do this is to keep a new Stress Diary from time to time.

Another way is to check yourself for signs of stress when major changes occur. Pay attention to your body, mind, and behavior. Then apply the knowledge and skills you have gained to take control of the situation. Talk to people who can listen and offer advice. Decide which stressors you can avoid or change. Ask yourself, "Am I thinking negative thoughts?" You know how to squelch them!

Find ways to relax, perhaps by taking up a hobby, by spending quiet time at home, or by getting together with friends. As Diego reminds other young people, "You can joke around. You can talk about other things besides things that cause stress."

It's important to take care of your body, too, to exercise, eat nutritious meals, and get enough sleep. Also, people of any age need to be alert to the signs of depression and anxiety and to get help for these problems.

Of course, you don't need to wait until you are under stress to take good care of yourself. It's wise to make such healthful practices as relaxation, exercise, and good nutrition a regular part of your life. These good habits will help to protect you against stress when it does occur.

A healthy way of life will provide other benefits as well. These include a strong, flexible body and plenty of energy to do the things you want to do. People who are in good shape have a trim, healthful appearance. They reduce their risk of ill health now and in years to come.

But despite your best efforts, there will be times when stress gets you down. You are going to get upset. You may even get sick. Learning to deal with stress takes time. These experiences will teach you more about the ways your body and mind respond to difficulties. They will help you be better prepared the next time a problem occurs.

You will learn, too, to recognize the good stress, the stress that pushes you to succeed. People who welcome life's challenges are often the healthiest. They are the ones who grow and develop at every age.

Having a fit mind and body will help you get the most from life, whatever the future brings.

For Further Reading

Benson, Herbert, M.D., et al. *The Wellness Book: The Comprehensive Guide to Maintaining Health and Treating Stress-Related Illness.* New York: Birch Lane Press, 1992.

Brody, Jane E. *Jane Brody's The New York Times Guide to Personal Health.* New York: Times Books, 1982.

Cooper, Kenneth H., M.D., M.P.H. *Kid Fitness: A Complete Shape-Up Program from Birth Through High School.* New York: Bantam Books, 1991.

Elkind, David. *The Hurried Child: Growing Up Too Fast Too Soon.* Reading, Massachusetts: Addison-Wesley Publishing Co., 1988.

Hanson, Peter G., M.D. *The Joy of Stress.* Kansas City, Missouri: Andrews, McMeel & Parker, 1986.

Helpful Facts About Depressive Disorders. Rockville, Maryland: U.S. Department of Health and Human Services, 1987.

Webb, Wilse. *Sleep: The Gentle Tyrant.* Boston: Anchor Press, 1991.

What to Do When a Friend Is Depressed: A Guide for Teenagers. Rockville, Maryland: U.S. Department of Health and Human Services.

You Are Not Alone: Facts About Mental Health and Mental Illness. Rockville, Maryland: National Institute of Mental Health, 1985.

Index

high school, starting 8
hobbies 39–40, 46, 59
homework 7, 31
hopelessness 50
hormones 14–16
hypothalamus 14

illness 9, 22, 43, 50, 59
imagination 22, 24, 31–32, 52
immunizations 45

jobs 7

lateness 22
laughter 40–41, 46
listening 30, 34
lungs 15

medical checkups 45, 53
medication 53
mental fitness 6, 10, 21, 58–60
mental fitness program 26, 31,
    36
moving 8, 16, 21
muscles 6, 15, 24, 40–41, 43, 51

negative thinking 18, 22–23,
    31–32, 36, 58
nervousness 14
nutrition 6, 24, 43–46, 59

obesity 43
overeating 45, 50

panic 10, 51
parents 7–8, 29–30, 50, 53–54
peer pressure 9, 35
phobias 51–52
physical fitness 41–46, 59–60
physical health 9
popularity 8, 16
poverty 9
protein-rich foods 44
psychiatrist 52
psychologist 52

quiet time 40, 59

racism 9
relaxation 18, 25, 33, 39–42,
    46, 59
resistance stage 17
responsibilities 7
running away 49
rushing 24–25

salt 45
schedule 30, 33
school 5–8, 13–14, 16, 22, 49,
    57
self esteem 23, 32, 36
sex 9
shyness 16
sleep 6, 16, 45, 50, 59
smoking 24, 45
social worker 52
sodium 45
sports 7
stomachache 7, 16, 24, 50
stress diary 24–26, 31, 58
stressors 15, 21–27
stress-related illness 9, 22–23,
    51, 59
stress response 6–7, 13–19,
    23, 41, 58
stretching 43
success 8, 32, 60
suicide 10, 49–50, 54

talking about problems 29–31,
    40, 53
teachers 53–54
tension 8, 24, 51
tests 22
therapist 49–54
thought stopping 31–32, 36
time management 33, 36
tiredness 18

violence 9

warm-up 42–43
working 7
worry 14